D0172504

101 Things®
To Do With
a Toaster Oven

101 Things® To Do With a Toaster Oven

BY
DONNA KELLY

GIBBS SMITH
TO ENRICH AND INSPIRE HUMANKIND
Salt Lake City | Charleston | Santa Fe | Santa Barbara

First Edition
13 12 11 10 09   10 9 8 7 6 5 4 3 2 1

Published by
Gibbs Smith
P.O. Box 667
Layton, Utah 84041

1-800.835.4993 orders
www.gibbs-smith.com

Printed and bound in Korea
Gibbs Smith books are printed on either recycled, 100% post-consumer waste, FSC-certified papers, or on paper produced from a 100% certified sustainable forest/controlled wood source.

Library of Congress Cataloging-in-Publication Data

Kelly, Donna.
101 things to do with a toaster oven / Donna Kelly. — 1st ed.
p. cm.
ISBN-13: 978-1-4236-0648-2
ISBN-10: 1-4236-0648-5
1. Toaster oven cookery. I. Title. II. Title: One hundred and one things to do with a toaster oven.
TX840.T63K45 2009
641.5'86—dc22

2009000473

To all those home cooks who,
despite busy lives, put fabulous
food on the table day after day.

CONTENTS

Hearty Main Dishes

Veggie Main Dishes

Desserts

HELPFUL HINTS & FACTS

1. Toaster ovens have come a very long way in the last few years. They are versatile, handy, quick, and economical.

2. Toaster ovens heat up much more quickly than full-sized ovens and cook more efficiently. They have many different settings such as toast, defrost, broil, bake, and convection bake—just to name a few.

3. Toaster ovens take up very little space and are easy to clean (many have crumb trays that slide out). They also use less energy and don't heat up the entire kitchen.

4. Use the front window on a toaster oven for close monitoring of cooking food without opening the door and losing heat.

5. The little ovens are portable and can be moved around the kitchen to a space convenient for whatever you are cooking.

6. The "toast" feature allows for even browning on both sides of food, compared to conventional ovens that can only broil from the top.

7. The recipes in this book were created using a 6-slice capacity toaster oven. Most recipes use baking pans, but a few call for placing the item to be cooked directly on the wire rack in the toaster oven.

8. It is helpful to have a variety of pans to use in the toaster oven. The recipes in this book may require a 6-cup muffin pan; mini muffin pan; 8 x 11-inch baking sheet; 9-inch square baking pan; 9-inch pie pan; oval 2 1/2-quart casserole dish; or 8- to 10-ounce ramekins.

APPETIZERS

PIZZA BITES

1 tube (8 ounces)	**refrigerator biscuits,** flaky style
1 cup	**marinara sauce**
2 tablespoons	**tomato paste**
18 slices	**pepperoni**
1/4–1/2 cup	**grated mozzarella cheese**
3 tablespoons	**finely grated Parmesan cheese**

Turn toaster oven to toast on darkest setting.

Separate 3 biscuits into layers, making 6 thin circles from each biscuit. Save remaining biscuits for another use. Bake the dough circles in a single layer in two batches on a baking sheet until golden brown and toasty. Watch carefully so as not to burn.

In a bowl, whisk together the marinara sauce and tomato paste. Spread 1 tablespoon sauce mixture on each toasted circle. Top with pepperoni and cheeses. Return to oven and toast until cheeses are melted and sauce is bubbly. Serve warm. Makes 18 appetizers.

BAKED BRIE IN A BREAD CRUST

1/2 cup	**raspberry jam**
1/4 cup	**fresh or frozen raspberries**
1 tablespoon	**fresh thyme leaves**
1/2 box (17 ounces)	**frozen puff pastry,** thawed
1 (14-ounce)	**Brie cheese,** 6 to 7 inches in diameter
1	**large egg,** mixed with 1 tablespoon water

Turn toaster oven to 375 degrees.

Stir jam, berries, and thyme in small bowl to blend. Lay sheet of pastry on lightly floured surface and roll out to a 12-inch square. Cut top rind off cheese; discard rind. Place cheese, cut side up, in center of pastry and spread raspberry mixture on cheese. Fold pastry corners up over cheese. Brush pastry with egg wash and then press seams together to seal.

Bake on a baking sheet for 35–40 minutes, or until golden brown. Let cool 15 minutes. Place baked cheese on a serving platter. Serve with crackers and toasted baguette slices. Makes 6–8 servings.

SPINACH ARTICHOKE DIP

1 jar (14 ounces)	**marinated artichoke hearts**
1 box (10 ounces)	**frozen chopped spinach**
1/2 cup	**grated Monterey Jack cheese**
1/2 cup	**grated Parmigiano-Romano cheese**
1 package (8 ounces)	**light cream cheese,** softened
1/2 cup	**light sour cream**
1 teaspoon	**salt**
1/2 teaspoon	**garlic powder**
	Tabasco sauce, to taste

Turn toaster oven to convection bake at 350 degrees (or bake at 375 degrees).

Drain artichoke hearts, reserving 1/4 cup liquid. Dice artichoke hearts and remove any tough pieces. Thaw spinach; squeeze and drain all liquid from spinach.

Stir all ingredients together, including 1/4 cup reserved liquid. Spread mixture in a 9-inch pie pan prepared with nonstick cooking spray.

Bake 25–30 minutes, or until bubbly and lightly browned on top. Serve on crackers or toasted baguette slices. Makes 6–8 servings.

TOMATO MOZZARELLA BRUSCHETTA

1 loaf	**baguette-style French bread** (about 3 inches in diameter)
2 cloves	**garlic,** peeled and cut in half
4 ounces	**fresh mozzarella**
2	**medium ripe tomatoes,** diced
1/4 cup	**diced fresh basil**
1 teaspoon	**extra virgin olive oil**
	salt and pepper

Turn toaster oven to toast on dark setting.

Slice bread into 6 (1/2-inch-thick) slices. Place directly on wire rack at top of toaster oven. Toast until lightly browned, about 2–3 minutes on each side.

Remove from oven and rub tops of toasted slices with cut side of garlic cloves.

Slice mozzarella into 1/4-inch-thick slices to fit the toasts. Lay a slice on top of each piece of toast. Mix tomatoes, basil, and oil and spread about 2 tablespoons over cheese. Sprinkle with salt and pepper to taste. Makes 6 servings.

PARMESAN PESTO TWISTS

1 sheet (10 x 14-inches)	**frozen puff pastry dough,** thawed
1/4 cup	**pesto**
1/4 cup	**grated Parmesan cheese**
1	**large egg,** mixed with 1 tablespoon water

Turn toaster oven to convection bake at 350 degrees (or bake at 400 degrees).

Place puff pastry on a flat surface and pierce every 2 inches with a fork. Spread pesto sauce over pastry sheet. Fold sheet in half widthwise and then roll out to 10 x 14 inches.

Sprinkle on cheese and pat with fingers so that cheese sticks to pastry. Cut into 1-inch strips.

Place half of the strips about 2 inches apart on a baking sheet, twisting like a rope, so that there is a twist every inch or so. Brush strips with egg mixture. Press ends of strips to adhere to pan so strips will not move during baking. Bake in oven, near the top, for 8–10 minutes, or until slightly puffed and golden brown. Repeat using remaining strips. Makes 10 twists.

SUN-DRIED TOMATO PINWHEELS

1 jar (6 ounces)	**sun-dried tomatoes in oil,** drained
4 ounces	**cream cheese,** softened
1 teaspoon	**garlic powder**
	Tabasco sauce, to taste
1 box (17 ounces)	**frozen puff pastry,** thawed

Turn toaster oven to convection bake at 375 degrees (or bake at 400 degrees).

Dice the tomatoes and mix with cream cheese, garlic powder, and Tabasco sauce.

Lay each sheet of puff pastry on a flat surface and spread half the tomato mixture over each, leaving 1 inch around the edges. Roll up jellyroll style starting with the wide side. Cut into 1/2-inch slices and place, spiral side up, on a baking sheet.

Bake in two batches for 12–15 minutes each, or until golden brown. Remove from oven and remove from pan immediately so bottoms won't burn. Makes 24 pinwheels.

THREE-CHEESE BITES

2 cups	**grated sharp cheddar cheese**
3/4 cup	**grated Parmesan cheese**
1/2 cup	**crumbled feta cheese**
4 tablespoons	**unsalted butter or margarine**
1 cup	**flour**
1/2 teaspoon	**cumin**
1/4 teaspoon	**pepper**
	Tabasco sauce, to taste
2 tablespoons	**minced flat-leaf parsley**

Turn toaster oven to convection bake at 375 degrees (or bake at 400 degrees).

Mix all ingredients together. Knead dough 10–12 times on a lightly floured surface, forming a ball.

Roll dough into 18 balls using about 1 tablespoon for each.

Place one ball per cup in a 6-cup muffin pan prepared with nonstick cooking spray. Bake in three batches for 15–18 minutes each, or until cooked through and golden brown. Makes 18 appetizers.

CRAB-STUFFED WONTONS

1 can (6 ounces)	**crabmeat,** drained
2 tablespoons	**cream cheese,** softened
1 tablespoon	**chili sauce**
1/2 cup	**diced red bell pepper**
1/4 cup	**thinly sliced green onions**
1/2 teaspoon	**lemon pepper seasoning**
16 (3 1/2-inch squares)	**refrigerated wonton wrappers**
1	**large egg,** mixed with 1 tablespoon water
1 tablespoon	**canola oil**

Turn toaster oven to convection bake at 350 degrees (or bake at 375 degrees).

Combine crab, cream cheese, chili sauce, bell pepper, onions, and seasoning. Lay out wonton wrappers and brush edges with egg wash. Place a generously mounded tablespoon of crab mixture in the center of each wonton. Fold each wonton in half, forming a triangle. Crimp edges with a fork.

Pour oil on an 8 x 11-inch baking sheet. Place wontons on baking sheet in a single layer. Brush tops with egg wash.

Bake for 8 minutes, then turn over and bake 5–8 minutes more, or until golden brown. Serve immediately with a teriyaki dipping sauce, if desired. Makes 16 appetizers.

ASIAN-STYLE CHICKEN WINGS

2 pounds	**chicken wing drumettes** (about 10–12 total)
1/2 cup	**cornstarch**
1/4 cup	**canola oil**
1/2 teaspoon	**lemon pepper seasoning**
1/2 teaspoon	**garlic powder**
2/3 cup	**sugar**
1/4 cup	**rice vinegar**
1/4 cup	**unsweetened pineapple juice**
1/4 cup	**ketchup**
2 tablespoons	**soy sauce**

Toss chicken in cornstarch. Saute in oil in a frying pan over medium-high heat, turning constantly for 3–5 minutes, or until lightly browned.

Meanwhile, in a small saucepan bring remaining ingredients to a boil and whisk until sugar is dissolved and sauce is thickened, about 3 minutes. Pour sauce over chicken and toss.

Turn toaster oven to bake at 375 degrees.

Place chicken in a single layer on an 8 x 11-inch baking sheet prepared with nonstick cooking spray and bake for about 30 minutes, turning over after 15 minutes. Serve hot. Makes 4–6 servings.

BREAKFAST

BREAKFAST PIZZA

1 tablespoon	**canola oil**
1 tube (8 ounces)	**refrigerated crescent rolls**
5	**large eggs**
1/2 box (9 ounces)	**fully cooked sausage links**
1/2 cup	**diced red bell pepper**
1/2 cup	**thinly sliced green onion,** some tops included
1/2 cup	**grated mozzarella or cheddar cheese**

Turn toaster oven to convection bake at 350 degrees (or bake at 375 degrees).

Pour oil evenly over bottom of an 8 x 11-inch baking pan. Unroll crescent dough and lay on pan, completely covering bottom in a single layer. Press with fingers to seal perforations and cover pan completely. Beat eggs and pour on top of dough, spreading evenly.

Slice sausage links into 1/4-inch slices and scatter over eggs. Sprinkle with bell pepper and green onion. Sprinkle cheese evenly over top.

Bake in center of toaster oven for 18–20 minutes, or until eggs are set and lightly browned. Serve immediately. Makes 4–6 servings.

TOASTER OVEN HASH BROWNS

1	**large russet or Yukon gold potato,** peeled
2 tablespoons	**canola oil,** divided
1 teaspoon	**salt**
1/2 teaspoon	**pepper**

Turn toaster oven to convection bake at 400 degrees (or bake at 425 degrees).

Place a 2-quart baking pan in the oven and heat for 10 minutes.

Meanwhile, grate the potato on the large holes of a box grater. Toss the grated potato with 1 tablespoon oil, salt, and pepper.

Remove pan from toaster oven and pour in remaining oil. Spread potato mixture in pan and then cover with aluminum foil.

Bake for 15 minutes. Remove pan, uncover, and return to oven and bake 5–8 minutes more, or until tops of potatoes begin to brown. Serve immediately. Makes 4 servings.

SAVORY SUNRISE SCONES

4 cups	**flour**
2 tablespoons	**baking powder**
2 teaspoons	**salt**
1/2 cup	**cold unsalted butter or margarine**
1 cup	**cream**
5	**large eggs,** divided
4 cups	**grated cheddar cheese**
1/2 cup	**thinly sliced green onions**
4 slices	**cooked bacon,** crumbled

Turn toaster oven to bake at 350 degrees.

In a large mixing bowl, combine the flour, baking powder, and salt. Using a pastry cutter, cut butter into mixture until small crumbs form.

Stir together cream and 4 eggs. With a hand mixer on medium speed, add cream mixture to dry mixture until just mixed together. Stir in cheese, onions, and bacon.

On a floured surface, roll out or pat dough to 1/2 inch thickness. Cut into circles or triangles about 4 inches in diameter. Mix the remaining egg with 1 tablespoon water. Brush scones with egg wash and place on a baking sheet prepared with nonstick cooking spray about 1/2 inch apart. Bake in batches for 20–25 minutes each, or until golden brown. Makes 16 scones.

GREEN EGGS AND HAM CUPS

2	**green onions,** thinly sliced
2 cloves	**garlic,** minced
1 tablespoon	**butter or margarine**
10 ounces	**frozen chopped spinach,** thawed and squeezed dry
1/2 cup	**light sour cream**
1 teaspoon	**salt**
1/4 teaspoon	**nutmeg**
8 slices	**ham lunchmeat**
8	**large eggs**
3/4 cup	**grated Parmesan cheese**

Turn toaster oven to bake at 375 degrees.

Cook onions and garlic in butter in a frying pan over medium heat for about 3 minutes, or until softened. Add the spinach, sour cream, salt, and nutmeg. Cook until most of the liquid has evaporated, about 3 minutes, stirring frequently.

Prepare 8 (8- to 10-ounce) ramekins with nonstick cooking spray. Line the ramekins with ham slices, making sure the entire surface of cup is covered. Spread 1/4 cup spinach mixture into bottom and slightly up sides of ham cup. Crack an egg into each cup. Sprinkle a little Parmesan cheese on top and then bake 4 ramekins at a time for 12–15 minutes, depending desired doneness. (Remember that the eggs will continue to cook for a few minutes after taking them out of the oven.) Remove from oven and carefully remove from ramekins and place on serving plates. Makes 8 servings.

APPLE POPOVER PANCAKE

2	**medium Granny Smith apples,** peeled and cored
4 tablespoons	**unsalted butter or margarine,** divided
4 tablespoons	**sugar,** divided
1/4 teaspoon	**cinnamon**
1/4 teaspoon	**nutmeg**
3	**large eggs**
3/4 cup	**milk**
3/4 cup	**flour**
1 teaspoon	**vanilla**
1/2 teaspoon	**salt**

Turn toaster oven to bake at 400 degrees; place a 9-inch pie pan in oven to preheat.

Saute the apples in 2 tablespoons butter in a medium frying pan over medium-high heat for about 2 minutes. Add 2 tablespoons sugar, cinnamon, and nutmeg. Cook another 3–5 minutes, or until apples are fork tender. Place apple mixture in the preheated pie pan.

Melt the remaining butter. Blend the melted butter, remaining sugar, and all remaining ingredients in a blender. Pour mixture over apples.

Bake for 20 minutes, making sure not to open oven door during cooking so pancake can properly "puff." Serve immediately with syrup or powdered sugar. Makes 4 servings.

LEMON POPPY SEED SCONES

3 cups	**flour**
1 cup	**sugar,** plus more for sprinkling
3 tablespoons	**poppy seeds**
1 tablespoon	**baking powder**
2 teaspoons	**lemon zest**
1 teaspoon	**salt**
10 tablespoons	**chilled unsalted butter**
1	**large egg**
2 tablespoons	**fresh lemon juice**
1/3 cup	**whole milk,** plus more for brushing
	sugar

Turn toaster oven to convection bake at 350 degrees (or bake at 375 degrees).

Mix together flour, sugar, poppy seeds, baking powder, lemon zest, and salt in a food processor or stand mixer. Add butter and cut in until mixture resembles small crumbs. Whisk egg and lemon juice in a medium bowl to blend. Add to flour mixture, processing until clumps form. Add milk, processing just until dough comes together, adding more milk if dough seems dry.

Using floured hands, gather dough into a ball and then flatten into an 8-inch circle. Cut into 8 pie-shaped wedges. Transfer scones to a baking sheet and brush with a little milk. Sprinkle with some sugar.

Bake on an 8 x 11-inch baking sheet until scones are golden brown, about 25 minutes. Transfer to a rack and cool. Makes 4–6 servings.

BREAKFAST BARS

2 cups	**granola cereal**
1 cup	**wheat nugget cereal,** such as Grape-Nuts
1 cup	**milk**
1 cup	**applesauce**
1 cup	**diced dried fruit**
1 teaspoon	**vanilla extract**

Turn toaster oven to bake at 350 degrees.

Mix all ingredients together and pour into a 9-inch square baking pan prepared with nonstick cooking spray.

Bake for 35–40 minutes, or until firm. Cool slightly. While still warm, cut into bars. Makes 6 servings.

PARMESAN-BAKED EGGS

3 tablespoons	**unsalted butter or margarine,** divided
1/4 cup	**finely grated Parmesan cheese,** divided
6	**large eggs**
1 teaspoon	**salt**
1/2 teaspoon	**pepper**
1 1/2 tablespoons	**minced flat-leaf parsley**

Turn toaster oven to bake at 400 degrees.

Spread 1/2 tablespoon butter in bottom and 1/2 inch up the sides of 6 (8- to 10-ounce) ramekins. Put 1 teaspoon Parmesan cheese in each ramekin and then turn and shake ramekin so the cheese coats the butter evenly.

Crack one egg into each ramekin. Sprinkle a little salt and pepper on top of each egg. Sprinkle each with 2 teaspoons cheese and then 2 teaspoons parsley.

Bake for 9–10 minutes for soft egg yolks, or 1–2 minutes longer for more firm yolks. Serve immediately. Makes 6 servings.

OPEN-FACED BREAKFAST SANDWICH

4 slices	**whole wheat or multigrain bread**
4	**large eggs**
2 tablespoons	**light sour cream**
1 tablespoon	**butter or margarine**
2 ounces	**Gouda or smoked Gouda cheese**
1/2 cup	**diced ham or cooked and diced sausage**
1/2 cup	**diced red onion**
1	**avocado,** thinly sliced

Turn toaster oven to toast on darkest setting.

Place bread slices directly on wire rack in toaster oven and toast for 3–5 minutes, or until lightly browned. Remove bread and then turn toaster oven to broil at 450 degrees.

Mix together eggs and sour cream and then scramble with butter in a medium frying pan.

Place slices of toast on a baking sheet. Thinly slice cheese to fit bread slices. Top each piece in the order of the following: cheese slices, scrambled eggs, ham, and onion. Broil for 5–8 minutes, watching closely so as not to burn. Remove from oven and cool a few minutes. Top with avocado slices and serve immediately. Makes 4 servings.

HUEVOS RANCHEROS STACKS

8	**corn tortillas**
4 tablespoons	**unsalted butter or margarine,** divided
1 can (14 ounces)	**red enchilada sauce**
1 can (6 ounces)	**tomato paste**
1 can (16 ounces)	**refried beans**
2 cups	**grated cheddar cheese**
4	**large eggs**

Turn toaster oven to broil at 450 degrees.

Saute each tortilla over medium-high heat in 1/2 tablespoon butter until cooked through but not crisp, about 30 seconds on each side.

Mix together enchilada sauce and tomato paste. Using 2 tablespoons sauce, make 2 small circles on a baking sheet. Layer on top of each circle the following: 1 tortilla, some refried beans, some cheese, more sauce, 1 tortilla, and more sauce. Press down each stack with a large spoon, making an indentation. Crack 1 egg on top of each stack into indentation.

Broil for 3–5 minutes, or until eggs reach desired doneness. Drizzle with more sauce and cheese. Repeat process again, making four total stacks. Serve immediately. Makes 4 servings.

GREAT START GRAPEFRUIT

2	**ruby red grapefruit**
4 teaspoons	**honey**
2 tablespoons	**finely minced crystallized ginger**
1/3 cup	**sugar**

Cut grapefruit in half and then cut a little of the skin off the round bottom of each in order to stabilize. Remove seeds.

Drizzle 1 teaspoon honey on top of each half. Sprinkle ginger on top. Spread sugar over top, pressing down with fingers so that most of sugar sinks into the grapefruit.

Broil on top rack of toaster oven for 10–15 minutes, or until sugar is browned and bubbly. Makes 4 servings.

HASH BROWN CASSEROLE

1 1/2 cups	**light sour cream**
2	**large eggs**
24 ounces	**frozen hash brown potatoes**
1 teaspoon	**seasoned salt**
1 cup	**thinly sliced green onions,** some tops included
2 cups	**grated cheddar cheese**
1 can (6 ounces)	**french-fried onions**

Turn toaster oven to bake at 350 degrees.

Combine sour cream and eggs and then mix together all ingredients except french-fried onions.

Spread mixture in a 2 1/2-quart baking dish that has been prepared with nonstick cooking spray. Sprinkle onions over top. Bake for 35–40 minutes, or until bubbly and golden brown. Makes 4–6 servings.

EGGS IN A BASKET

8	**large eggs,** divided
1/2 cup	**milk**
1/2 teaspoon	**garlic powder**
1/2 teaspoon	**salt**
6 slices	**day-old firm bread,** crusts removed
1 cup	**grated cheddar or Monterey Jack cheese**

Turn toaster oven to bake at 400 degrees.

Prepare 6 (8- to 10-ounce) ramekins generously with nonstick cooking spray. Mix 2 eggs, milk, garlic powder, and salt in a pie pan. Dip bread slices for 10 seconds on each side, then press one soaked bread slice lightly into each ramekin, forming a "basket."

Crack one of the remaining eggs into each of the six baskets. Sprinkle a little cheese on top and then bake for 15 minutes for slightly soft centers or cook longer for more firm centers. Makes 6 servings.

SANDWICHES & LUNCHES

WEEKNIGHT CALZONES

4 cups	**diced vegetables,** such as mushrooms, onions, broccoli, or zucchini
	oil
1 loaf (8 ounces)	**frozen bread dough,** thawed
1 tablespoon	**minced fresh garlic**
1 cup	**marinara sauce**
2 cups	**grated mozzarella cheese**
3/4 cup	**grated Parmesan cheese**
1 can (4 ounces)	**sliced black olives**
4 ounces	**Canadian bacon or pepperoni,** diced
4 tablespoons	**extra virgin olive oil,** divided

Turn toaster oven to convection bake at 400 degrees (or bake at 425 degrees).

Saute vegetables for a few minutes in a little oil until just tender.

Cut bread dough loaf into fourths and form each piece into a ball. Roll each ball into a flat 8- to 10-inch circle.

Mix garlic into marinara sauce. On half of each circle, spread 1/4 cup sauce, leaving a 1/2 inch around the edge. On top of sauce, place 1 cup vegetables, 1/2 cup mozzarella cheese, 2 tablespoons Parmesan cheese, olives, and some meat.

Fold each dough half over filling to form a semicircle; pinch closed all the way around. Brush each calzone with 1/2 tablespoon olive oil.

Pour remaining oil on a baking sheet. Bake for 15–18 minutes, or until lightly browned on top. Makes 4 servings.

SIMPLE SAMOSAS

1/2	**medium yellow onion,** diced
1 tablespoon	**olive oil**
1 pound	**lean ground beef**
1/4 cup	**slivered almonds**
1/2 cup	**ketchup**
1/4 cup	**diced raisins**
1 tablespoon	**apple cider vinegar**
1 teaspoon	**curry powder**
1/2 teaspoon	**allspice**
1/2 teaspoon	**salt**
	Tabasco sauce, to taste
1 tube (8 ounces)	**refrigerated jumbo buttermilk biscuits**
1	**large egg,** mixed with 1 tablespoon water

Turn toaster oven to bake at 375 degrees.

Saute onion in oil in a large frying pan over medium-high heat for 2 minutes. Add ground beef and saute until cooked through, breaking into small bits. Turn off heat and stir in almonds, ketchup, raisins, vinegar, spices, and Tabasco sauce.

On a flat, floured surface, roll out each biscuit to a 6-inch circle, about 1/4 inch thick. Mound 2 tablespoons meat mixture on one half of each biscuit circle. Brush edges with egg wash. Fold dough over meat mixture to make a half circle and seal and crimp edges with a fork.

Place on a baking sheet prepared with nonstick cooking spray. Bake for 12–15 minutes, or until lightly browned. Serve immediately. Makes 6 servings.

REUBEN BRATWURST ROLLS

4	**large hoagie rolls**
4 tablespoons	**spicy brown mustard**
4	**cooked bratwurst sausages**
2 cups	**sauerkraut**
4 slices	**Swiss cheese**

Turn toaster oven to toast on darkest setting.

Open hoagie rolls and place directly on wire rack in toaster oven. Toast for 5–8 minutes, or until lightly toasted. Remove rolls and then turn toaster oven to broil at 450 degrees.

Spread bottoms of hoagie rolls with mustard. Cut sausages in half lengthwise and place on rolls. Spoon sauerkraut evenly over top. Lay cheese slices over top.

Place rolls on an 8 x 11-inch baking sheet. Broil for 5–8 minutes, watching closely so as not to burn, until heated through and cheese is melted. Makes 4 servings.

SOUTHERN-STYLE CHICKEN AND WAFFLES

4	**frozen waffles** (5 inches in diameter)
2 tablespoons	**unsalted butter or margarine**
2 tablespoons	**flour**
1 1/2 cups	**half-and-half**
1/2 teaspoon	**salt**
1 teaspoon	**cracked black pepper**
1/4 teaspoon	**nutmeg**
2 cups	**shredded rotisserie chicken,** warm
2	**green onions,** thinly sliced, tops included

Turn toaster oven to toast on dark setting.

Place waffles directly on racks in middle of toaster oven. Cook for about 5 minutes, or until crisp and browned.

Meanwhile, melt butter in a frying pan over medium heat. Stir in flour and let cook 1–2 minutes. Slowly whisk in half-and-half and whisk 1–2 minutes, simmering a few minutes until thickened. Stir in salt, pepper, and nutmeg.

Layer on each serving plate in the following order: 1 waffle, 2 tablespoons sauce, 1/2 cup chicken, 1/4 cup sauce drizzled over chicken, and a few sprinkles of green onion. Serve immediately. Makes 4 servings.

HAM AND CHEESE STROMBOLIS

2 tubes (10 ounces each)	**refrigerated pizza dough**
1/2 cup	**finely grated Parmesan cheese**
4 ounces	**thinly sliced deli ham**
8 ounces	**thinly sliced Provolone cheese**
2 cups	**chopped fresh spinach**
1	**egg,** beaten with 1 tablespoon water

Turn toaster oven to toast on darkest setting.

Unroll pizza dough, forming two rectangles about 8 x 12 inches each.

Sprinkle Parmesan cheese evenly over rectangles. Lay ham slices on top, forming a single layer. Lay Provolone slices on top, forming a single layer. Sprinkle spinach over top. Roll up each rectangle, jellyroll style, from widest side of rectangle. Cut each roll in half, forming 4 rolls. Brush each roll with egg mixture.

Bake rolls, two at a time, in toaster oven for 15–18 minutes, or until golden brown. Serve immediately. Makes 4 servings.

TURKEY AVOCADO MELTS

1 loaf (16 ounces)	**ciabatta or foccacia bread,** or 8 slices whole wheat bread
8 ounces	**garden vegetable cream cheese**
8 ounces	**thinly sliced deli turkey**
2 cups	**grated Monterey Jack or pepper jack cheese**
1	**avocado,** thinly sliced
3	**tomatoes,** thinly sliced

Turn toaster oven to toast on darkest setting.

Place bread on the counter and, with a large knife parallel to the counter, slice bread in half, forming two rectangles about 8 x 12 inches each.

Spread cream cheese evenly over rectangles. Lay turkey slices on top, forming a single layer. Sprinkle cheese over top.

Bake each rectangle one at a time, in toaster oven for 5–8 minutes, or until cheese is bubbly and golden brown. Lay avocado and tomato slices on top, forming a single layer. Serve immediately. Makes 4–6 servings.

CLASSIC TUNA MELTS

1 can (6 ounces)	**albacore tuna in water,** drained
2 tablespoons	**light cream cheese**
1 teaspoon	**Dijon mustard**
1 tablespoon	**lemon juice**
2 tablespoons	**minced fresh parsley**
1 1/2 cups	**grated Gruyère or Monterey Jack cheese**
3/4 cup	**grated Parmesan cheese**
6 slices	**white or whole grain bread**

Turn toaster oven to toast on darkest setting.

Mix together all ingredients except bread. Spread each slice of bread with tuna mixture.

Place slices of bread, two at a time, directly on wire rack in toaster oven. Cook 5–8 minutes, or until bread is toasted on bottom and browned and bubbly on top. Serve immediately. Makes 6 servings.

HOT CHICKEN SALAD

2 cups	**1-inch cubes chicken**
1/2 cup	**light sour cream**
1/2 cup	**mayonnaise**
1 tablespoon	**lemon juice**
2 ribs	**celery,** diced
1 can (4 ounces)	**sliced mushrooms,** drained and diced
2	**green onions,** thinly sliced, tops included
1/2 cup	**crushed butter-flavored crackers**
1/2 cup	**sliced almonds**
4 cups	**cooked rice**

Turn toaster oven to bake at 375 degrees.

Stir all ingredients together except almonds and rice. Spread mixture in a 2 1/2-quart baking dish that has been generously prepared with nonstick cooking spray. Bake for 20 minutes. Sprinkle almonds on top and bake another 15–20 minutes, or until bubbly and golden brown. Serve over cooked rice. Makes 4–6 servings.

TWICE-BAKED POTATOES

3	**large russet or Yukon gold potatoes**
2 cups	**grated sharp cheddar cheese**
1/2 cup	**light sour cream**
3	**green onions,** thinly sliced
1/2 cup	**real bacon bits,** optional
1/2 teaspoon	**salt**
1/2 teaspoon	**pepper**
3/4 cup	**grated Parmesan cheese**

Turn toaster oven to bake at 400 degrees.

Place potatoes directly on wire rack in toaster oven and bake for 1 hour. Remove from oven and cool to warm.

Slice potatoes in half lengthwise. Scoop out most of flesh with a spoon; reserve 1 1/2 cups of flesh and set potato skins aside. Mix reserved potato flesh with cheddar cheese, sour cream, onions, bacon, salt, and pepper. Fill potato skins with mixture, mounding slightly on top. Sprinkle with Parmesan cheese.

Turn toaster oven to broil at 450 degrees.

Place filled potato halves directly on wire rack near top of oven and broil for 8–10 minutes, or until browned and bubbly. Serve immediately. Makes 6 servings.

PITA PIZZAS

6	**round pita breads**
	spray canola oil
1 1/2 cups	**marinara sauce**
1 can (4 ounces)	**tomato paste**
3 cups	**grated mozzarella cheese**
	pizza toppings, such as pepperoni, sausage, sliced olives, and sliced mushrooms
3/4 cup	**grated Parmesan cheese**

Turn toaster oven to toast on the darkest setting.

Place 2 pita rounds at a time directly on wire rack in oven and toast for 3–5 minutes, or until lightly browned on both sides. Spray tops of toasted pita rounds lightly with oil.

Mix together the marinara sauce and tomato paste. Spread 1/3 cup on each pita round. Sprinkle a little mozzarella cheese over top. Spread desired toppings on each pita round and then sprinkle a little Parmesan cheese over top.

Turn toaster oven to broil at 450 degrees.

Cook pizzas directly on wire rack of toaster oven, with two at a time in the oven for 5–8 minutes, or until bottom of pitas are toasted and tops are bubbly and lightly browned. Serve immediately. Makes 6 servings.

TOASTER OVEN CHEESE SANDWICHES

8 slices	**bread**
4 tablespoons	**unsalted butter or margarine,** melted
1 teaspoon	**seasoned salt**
2 cups	**grated medium cheddar cheese**
3/4 cup	**grated Gruyère or smoked Gouda cheese**

Turn toaster oven to toast on darkest setting.

Brush one side of each slice of bread with butter and then sprinkle with seasoned salt. Turn four of the slices over with buttered side facing down. Spread 1/4 of each cheese on top of those four slices. Place other slices of bread, buttered sides up, on top of cheese.

Place directly on wire rack near top of toaster oven. Cook until both sides are golden brown, about 8–10 minutes. Makes 4 servings.

BAKED MAC 'N' CHEESE

16 ounces	**elbow macaroni**
3 cups	**whole milk**
$^1/_3$ cup	**flour**
6 cups	**grated sharp cheddar cheese**
$^3/_4$ cup	**grated Parmesan cheese**
1 teaspoon	**seasoned salt,** or more to taste
$^1/_2$ cup	**breadcrumbs**

Boil macaroni in salted water according to package directions; drain and set aside.

Turn toaster oven to bake at 375 degrees.

Blend the milk and flour together in a blender. Bring milk mixture to a simmer in a medium saucepan. Simmer for about 5 minutes, or until thickened. Slowly add cheeses, stirring until blended. Stir in seasoned salt to taste. Stir cheese mixture into cooked macaroni and then spread in a 2$^1/_2$-quart baking dish that has been prepared with nonstick cooking spray. Sprinkle breadcrumbs on top.

Bake for 15–20 minutes, or until cooked through and bubbly. Serve immediately. Makes 4–6 servings.

HARVEST MEDLEY ACORN SQUASH

3	**acorn squash**
1 box (6 ounces)	**wild rice mix,** any flavor
2 1/4 cups	**reduced-sodium chicken or vegetable broth**
2 teaspoons	**white wine vinegar**
3 tablespoons	**pure maple syrup,** divided
1/2 cup	**diced yellow onion**
1/2 cup	**diced Golden Delicious apple**
3 tablespoons	**unsalted butter or margarine,** melted and divided
1/2 cup	**diced toasted hazelnuts or pecans**
1/2 cup	**dried cranberries,** diced

Cut each squash in half across the diameter. Scoop out seeds and strings. Boil in salted water for 5 minutes. Remove from water and place on a baking sheet prepared with nonstick cooking spray, cut side facing up. Slice piece off bottom if needed to stabilize.

Bring rice mix with seasoning packet to a simmer with broth, vinegar, and 1 tablespoon maple syrup. Cover and simmer for 15 minutes. Remove from heat and let stand uncovered. Meanwhile, saute onion and apple over medium-high heat in 1 tablespoon butter for 1–2 minutes, or until softened. Stir onion and apple into rice mixture with the hazelnuts and cranberries.

Turn toaster oven to bake at 375 degrees.

Spoon rice mixture into squash halves. Stir remaining butter and maple syrup together. Drizzle syrup mixture over squash. Bake for 25–30 minutes, or until lightly browned. Makes 6 servings.

RUSTIC SPINACH PIE

2 boxes (10 ounces each)	**frozen chopped spinach,** thawed
1 sheet (10 inches)	**refrigerated pie crust**
3 cloves	**garlic,** minced
6 ounces	**feta cheese,** crumbled
6	**large eggs,** divided
1 cup	**half-and-half**
1/2 teaspoon	**salt**
1/4 teaspoon	**nutmeg**

Turn toaster oven to bake at 400 degrees.

Squeeze the spinach dry with a kitchen towel. Lay the pie crust on a flat surface. Spread spinach evenly over top, leaving 2 inches around edge of crust bare. Sprinkle garlic and feta over top. Bring edge of crust up over spinach mixture, forming a crust about 1 inch deep all around. Crack one of the eggs and mix together with 1 tablespoon water. Brush crust edge with egg mixture. Mix together the remainder of the egg mixture, remaining eggs, half-and-half, salt, and nutmeg. Pour over spinach mixture. Bake for 30–35 minutes, or until filling is set and crust is golden brown. Serve immediately. Makes 4–6 servings.

TURKEY SALSA ROLLS

6 (1/8-inch-thick) slices	**turkey breast**
6 slices	**Monterey Jack or pepper jack cheese**
1/2 cup	**thinly sliced green onions**
1 cup	**salsa**
1 cup	**crumbled queso fresco cheese***

Turn toaster oven to broil at 450 degrees.

Lay turkey slices flat and place a slice of cheese and some green onions on top. Roll up, jellyroll style, from short edge. Broil for 3–5 minutes, or until turkey is browned and cheese is melted. Remove from oven and top each roll with some salsa and queso fresco. Makes 4–6 servings.

*If queso fresco cheese is not available, use cottage cheese that has been rinsed, drained, and mashed with a fork.

HAM AND ASPARAGUS ROLLS

12	**medium asparagus stalks**
1 1/2 cups	**grated Swiss or Havarti cheese**
1 cup	**flour,** divided
1/4 teaspoon	**nutmeg**
6 (1/8-inch-thick) slices	**ham**
2 cups	**cooked rice**
1	**large egg,** mixed with 1 tablespoon water
1 cup	**panko or breadcrumbs**

Turn toaster oven to convection bake at 400 degrees (or bake at 425 degrees).

Place asparagus on a plate, cover with plastic wrap, and microwave for about 1 minute, or until fork tender.

Toss cheese with 1/2 tablespoon flour and nutmeg. Lay the ham slices on a flat surface. Place 2 asparagus stalks lengthwise on each ham slice with a little of the cheese mixture. Spread 1/3 cup rice on top of each, and then roll ham slices up, beginning with short end. Roll the ham rolls first in flour, then in egg wash, then in panko or breadcrumbs. Bake on a baking sheet prepared with nonstick cooking spray for 5–8 minutes, or until browned. Makes 6 servings.

SNACKS & MORE

RUSTIC CHEESE CRACKERS

8 ounces	**sharp cheddar cheese,** diced
1/2 cup	**flour**
1/2 cup	**whole wheat flour**
1/4 teaspoon	**salt**
1/4 teaspoon	**white pepper**
1/4 teaspoon	**garlic powder**
3 tablespoons	**olive oil**
1/3 cup	**very finely minced or ground walnuts or pecans**
1/4 cup	**water**

Process all ingredients in a food processor until small crumbs form. Roll dough into 2 logs, each about 3 inches in diameter. Wrap with plastic wrap and refrigerate for at least 1 hour or overnight.

Turn toaster oven to convection bake at 350 degrees (or bake at 375 degrees).

Cut the dough into 1/4-inch-thick slices and place in a single layer on a baking sheet that has been covered with parchment paper or a silicone baking mat. Bake in two batches for 12–15 minutes, or until crackers are golden brown. Remove pan from toaster oven and slide the parchment paper or mat off the pan immediately. Allow to cool and serve as you would regular crackers. Makes about 24 crackers.

CRUSTY CHEESE BREAD

1 1/2 cups	**flour**
2 teaspoons	**baking powder**
1/4 teaspoon	**cayenne pepper**
1/2 teaspoon	**salt**
2/3 cup	**whole or 2 percent milk**
1 tablespoon	**unsalted butter or margarine,** melted
1	**large egg**
1/4 cup	**sour cream**
1 tablespoon	**olive oil**
2 ounces	**sharp cheddar cheese**
1/2 cup	**grated Parmesan cheese**

Turn toaster oven to bake at 350 degrees.

Stir together flour, baking powder, cayenne, and salt. Whisk together milk, butter, egg, and sour cream. Stir wet ingredients into dry ingredients, just until moistened.

Pour olive oil into a 9-inch square baking pan. Pour batter into pan. Cut cheddar cheese into small cubes. Sprinkle cubes over top of batter. Sprinkle Parmesan cheese over top. Press cheese down into batter. Bake for 30 minutes. Serve warm from oven, cut into squares. Makes 6 servings.

ENGLISH MUFFIN PIZZAS

3	**English muffins,** split in half
	spray canola oil
1 jar (16 ounces)	**pizza sauce**
	pepperoni and other favorite pizza toppings
1 1/2 cups	**grated mozzarella cheese**
3/4 cup	**grated Parmesan cheese**

Turn toaster oven to toast on darkest setting.

Place muffins directly on wire racks and toast until lightly browned, about 3–5 minutes.

Remove toasted slices, spray each with a little canola oil and place on an 8 x 11-inch baking sheet. Top with a little pizza sauce and then remaining ingredients as desired. Bake for about 5 minutes more, or until bubbly and browned. Makes 3–4 servings.

TOASTER OVEN NACHOS

1 bag (10 ounces)	**corn tortilla chips**
1 cup	**grated pepper jack cheese**
1	**cooked boneless, skinless chicken breast,** diced
1 teaspoon	**salt**
1 teaspoon	**chipotle chile powder**
1 cup	**corn**
2	**green onions,** thinly sliced, tops included
1	**avocado,** peeled and chopped
1 can (4 ounces)	**diced green chiles**
2 tablespoons	**fresh lime juice**
1/4 cup	**sour cream**
1 1/2 cups	**crumbled queso fresco cheese***
1/4 cup	**diced cilantro**

Turn toaster oven to broil at 450 degrees.

Arrange chips in a single layer on an 8 x 11-inch baking pan with edges. Sprinkle over chips in the following order: pepper jack cheese, chicken, salt, chile powder, corn, and green onions. Place on middle rack in oven and broil 3–5 minutes, watching closely so as not to burn.

Meanwhile, in a blender, blend avocado, green chiles, lime juice, and sour cream.

Remove nachos from oven and drizzle avocado sauce over nachos. Sprinkle queso fresco and cilantro over top. Serve immediately. Makes 4 servings.

*If queso fresco cheese is not available, use cottage cheese that has been rinsed, drained, and mashed with a fork.

SWEET POTATO OVEN FRIES

1	**large sweet potato or yam,** peeled
2 tablespoons	**canola oil**
1 teaspoon	**seasoned salt**
1 teaspoon	**cumin**
1/2 teaspoon	**garlic powder**
1/2 teaspoon	**onion powder**

Turn toaster oven to convection bake at 375 degrees (or bake at 400 degrees).

Cut sweet potato into planks about 1/2 inch thick and 1 inch wide. Toss planks in oil.

Mix together salt and spices. Spread oiled sweet potato on an 8 x 11-inch baking sheet and sprinkle with half of the spice mixture. Bake for 20 minutes, remove from oven, and turn over. Sprinkle with remaining spice mixture and return to oven to 8–10 minutes more, or until cooked through and browned. Makes 4–6 servings.

TOASTER OVEN S'MORES

8	**graham crackers**
4 tablespoons	**Nutella spread**
4	**chocolate bars**
8	**large marshmallows**

Turn toaster oven to broil at 450 degrees.

Spread 4 graham crackers with chocolate spread. Place desired amount of chocolate bar pieces on top of the chocolate spread. Put 2 marshmallows on top of the chocolate.

Place the s'mores on an 8 x 11-inch baking sheet and slide into the toaster oven. Broil for about 2 minutes, or until the marshmallows begin to brown. Remove and let cool for a few seconds. Top with remaining graham crackers. Makes 4 servings.

SWEET AND SPICY TOASTER OVEN NUTS

12 ounces	**mixed cashews, pecans, and walnuts** (about 2 cups nuts)
1 tablespoon	**unsalted butter or margarine**
2 tablespoons	**brown sugar**
1/2 teaspoon	**chili powder**
1/2 teaspoon	**allspice**
1/2 teaspoon	**cumin**
1/4 teaspoon	**salt**
1 tablespoon	**sugar**

Turn toaster oven to toast at darkest setting.

Roast nuts on a dry 8 x 11-inch baking sheet for 3–5 minutes, or until well heated and lightly browned.

Remove pan from toaster oven, pour nuts into a bowl and stir in butter. Toss in brown sugar, spices, and salt. Spread on a sheet of parchment or wax paper. Sprinkle with sugar and let cool. Makes 2 cups.

GARLIC CAESAR CROUTONS

4 cups	**1/2-inch cubes French bread**
	olive oil spray
2 teaspoons	**garlic powder**
1/2 teaspoon	**salt**
2 tablespoons	**finely grated Parmesan cheese**

Turn toaster oven to broil at 450 degrees.

Spread bread cubes on an 8 x 11-inch baking sheet in a single layer. Spray with olive oil until lightly coated. Combine the garlic powder, salt, and cheese. Sprinkle half of the mixture over bread cubes. Broil for 3–5 minutes, or until lightly browned. Turn bread cubes over and spray with oil and sprinkle the remaining mixture over top. Broil 2–3 minutes more, or until lightly browned. Makes 4 cups.

EASY CHEESY QUESADILLAS

2 cups **grated sharp cheddar cheese**
2 cups **grated Monterey Jack cheese**
8 **small flour tortillas** (6 to 7 inch diameter)
1 cup **diced green onions, green chiles, or any color bell pepper**

Turn toaster oven to toast at darkest setting.

Toss cheeses together in a bowl. Spread about 1/2 cup cheese evenly over 4 tortillas. Sprinkle about 1/4 cup onion or peppers over cheese. Place remaining tortillas on top of each and press down with your hand. Place quesadillas, one at a time, directly on wire rack in middle of toaster oven. Bake for 5–6 minutes, or until tortillas are browned and cheese is melted. Makes 4 servings.

SHORTCUT ELEPHANT EARS

1 tube (8 ounces)	**refrigerator crescent rolls**
2 tablespoons	**butter or margarine,** melted
2 tablespoons	**sugar**
1/2 teaspoon	**cinnamon**

Turn toaster oven to convection bake at 350 degrees (or bake at 375 degrees).

Remove dough from tube but do not unroll. Cut dough into 16 slices, about 1/2 inch thick each. Place slices on an 8 x 11-inch baking sheet about 2 inches apart, cut side up. (You will need to bake the slices in batches, to allow for rising while cooking.) Brush slices with butter. Stir sugar and cinnamon together. Sprinkle dough slices with half of the cinnamon sugar.

Bake for 10–12 minutes, or until golden brown. Remove from oven and immediately sprinkle with remaining sugar mixture. Cool to room temperature and serve. Makes 16 servings.

HONEY NUT SPIRALS

8 sheets	**frozen phyllo dough,** thawed
	spray olive oil
1/4 cup	**sugar**
1/2 teaspoon	**cinnamon**
1/4 teaspoon	**nutmeg**
1/4 cup	**honey,** divided
1/2 cup	**minced or ground walnuts,** divided
3 tablespoons	**unsalted butter or margarine,** melted

Turn toaster oven to convection bake at 350 degrees (or bake at 375 degrees).

Place 1 sheet of phyllo on a flat surface. Spray generously with olive oil. Repeat this 3 times so there are 4 sheets of phyllo with oil, then stack.

Stir together the sugar, cinnamon, and nutmeg. Sprinkle 2 tablespoons of sugar mixture on oiled phyllo stack. Drizzle 2 tablespoons honey on top. Sprinkle 1/4 cup walnuts over honey.

Top with another stack of four sheets of phyllo with oil on each sheet. Sprinkle on remaining sugar mixture, honey, and walnuts. Roll jellyroll style from the wide edge. Slice into 1/2-inch wide slices. Place slices spiral side up on an 8 x 11-inch baking sheet prepared with nonstick cooking spray. Brush with melted butter. Bake for 25–30 minutes, or until browned. Makes 18 spirals.

PARMESAN CRISPS

1 block (8 ounces)	**Parmesan cheese**
1 tablespoon	**flour**
1 teaspoon	**garlic powder**
1/2 teaspoon	**black pepper**

Turn toaster oven to convection bake at 375 degrees (or bake at 400 degrees).

Using large holes on grater, grate the cheese. Toss cheese with remaining ingredients.

Line an 8 x 11-inch baking sheet with parchment paper or a silicone mat. Place Parmesan mixture in four mounds of 1 tablespoon each on top of paper or mat. Spread each mound with the back of a spoon into a circle 3–4 inches wide. Parmesan bits should be in a single layer, with some thin gaps in between.

Bake near top of oven for 5–8 minutes, watching closely so as not to burn, until circles are lightly browned. Remove from toaster oven and slide paper or mat off baking sheet and onto counter. Let cool for 3–5 minutes. Can be left whole as a disc or can be broken up into bits. Repeat process until all remaining Parmesan is used. Use as a garnish on salads or soups, or with toppings as you would with crackers. Makes 16 crisps.

MIX 'N' MATCH MUFFINS

1 cup	**flour**
1 tablespoon	**baking powder**
1/2 teaspoon	**salt**
1/2 cup	**milk**
2 tablespoons	**sour cream**
1/2 cup	**sugar**
1/4 to 1/2 cup	**any diced fruit or nuts**
1/4 to 1/2 teaspoon	**cinnamon,** or any other spice as desired

Turn toaster oven to convection bake at 400 degrees (or bake at 425 degrees).

Stir all ingredients together. Do not over mix. Prepare a muffin pan with nonstick cooking spray. Fill muffin cups three-fourths full. Bake for 12–15 minutes, or until golden brown. Let cool to warm. Makes 6 muffins.

PARMESAN SPICE SOUP TOPPERS

4 slices	**dense white bread**
2 tablespoons	**unsalted butter or margarine,** melted
3 tablespoons	**finely grated Parmesan cheese**
1 tablespoon	**favorite ground spice** (such as cumin, paprika, chile powder, etc.)

Turn toaster oven to toast at darkest setting.

Cut shapes out of bread slices, such as stars, hearts, or squares. Brush both sides of bread shapes with a little butter. Spread cheese on a small plate. Press both sides of shapes into cheese. Place shapes in a single layer on an 8 x 11-inch baking sheet that has been covered with parchment paper. Toast in oven for 5–10 minutes, watching closely so as not to burn. Bread should be toasted and cheese should be lightly browned. Remove from oven and slide parchment paper off, sprinkle with spice as desired. Serve on top of a favorite bowl of soup. These are especially good on tomato soup or smooth creamed soups.

MEXICAN PIZZAS

4	**medium flour tortillas** (7 to 8 inch diameter)
2 cups	**grated cheddar cheese**
	salt and pepper
1 can (4 ounces)	**diced green chiles,** drained
1 can (6 ounces)	**sliced black olives,** drained
1/2 cup	**salsa**

Turn toaster oven to toast on darkest setting.

One at a time, place tortillas directly on wire rack in oven and toast until lightly browned on both sides, about 3 minutes each.

Turn toaster oven to broil at 450 degrees.

Place a crisp tortilla on an 8 x 11-inch baking sheet and sprinkle on a little of all of the remaining ingredients in the order listed above. Broil until cheese is melted and bubbly, about 5 minutes, watching closely so as not to burn. Repeat with remaining tortillas. Serve in wedges. Makes 4 servings.

TOASTER OVEN GARLIC BREAD

3 cloves	**garlic**
1 teaspoon	**salt**
4 tablespoons	**unsalted butter,** at room temperature
2 tablespoons	**finely grated Parmesan cheese**
1 tablespoon	**dried parsley flakes**
6 slices (1-inch each)	**French bread**

Turn toaster oven to toast on darkest setting.

Place garlic cloves on a cutting board and smash flat with the surface of a large sturdy knife. Sprinkle salt on top of garlic. Smash salt into garlic until it becomes a paste. Stir garlic paste together with butter, cheese, and parsley flakes. Spread mixture in a thin layer on one side of each bread slice.

Place bread slices, butter sides up, directly on wire rack near top of oven. Toast for 5–8 minutes, or until lightly browned. Serve immediately. Makes 6 servings.

HEARTY MAIN DISHES

MINI CHICKEN MEATLOAVES

1 1/2 pounds	**ground chicken**
2	**large eggs,** beaten
2 tablespoons	**sour cream**
1 tablespoon	**Dijon mustard**
1	**small yellow onion,** peeled and diced
1	**small Golden Delicious apple,** peeled, cored, and diced
2 cups	**fresh breadcrumbs**
3 tablespoons	**finely grated Parmesan cheese**
2 tablespoons	**minced flat-leaf parsley**
1/2 teaspoon	**salt**
1/2 teaspoon	**pepper**
	spray canola oil

Turn toaster oven to bake at 350 degrees.

Mix all ingredients except cooking spray together. Divide mixture into six equal parts. Shape into oblong loaf shapes. Spray loaves generously with cooking spray. Place on an 8 x 11-inch baking sheet prepared with nonstick cooking spray and bake for 30–35 minutes, or until golden brown. Serve immediately. Makes 6 servings.

HEAVENLY HALIBUT

4	**halibut fillets or steaks**
1/2 cup	**mayonnaise**
2 tablespoons	**flour**
1 tablespoon	**minced green onion tops**
1/4 cup	**sour cream**
1 tablespoon	**lemon juice**
1/2 teaspoon	**cayenne pepper**
3/4 cup	**grated Gruyère or Parmesan cheese**

Turn toaster oven to convection bake at 400 degrees (or bake at 425 degrees).

Pat halibut pieces dry with a paper towel. Arrange in a 9-inch square baking pan prepared with nonstick cooking spray.

Combine remaining ingredients except cheese. Spread mixture evenly over halibut. Sprinkle with cheese. Bake for 20–25 minutes, or until fish is cooked through and cheese is lightly browned. Makes 4 servings.

CHICKEN ENCHILADA STACKS

12	**corn tortillas**
3 tablespoons	**unsalted butter or margarine**
2 cups	**shredded rotisserie chicken**
1/2 tablespoon	**cumin**
1/2 tablespoon	**chile powder**
1 can (4 ounces)	**diced green chiles**
3	**green onions,** thinly sliced, tops included
1 cup	**corn**
1 can (28 ounces)	**red enchilada sauce**
1/2 cup	**salsa**
2 tablespoons	**flour**
4 cups	**grated sharp cheddar cheese**

Turn toaster oven to convection bake at 350 degrees (or bake at 375 degrees).

In a frying pan, saute tortillas one at a time in a little butter over medium-high heat until cooked through but not crisp, about 30 seconds on each side.

Place chicken in a bowl and stir together with cumin, chile powder, chiles, onions, and corn.

In a separate bowl, stir enchilada sauce, salsa, and flour together. Lay 4 tortillas on an 8 x 11-inch baking sheet prepared with nonstick cooking spray. Spread a little chicken mixture over each tortilla. Sprinkle some of the cheese over chicken and then pour some sauce over top. Repeat this process to make a second layer. Finish with a tortilla, a thin layer of enchilada sauce and a little cheese on top of each stack. Bake for 35–40 minutes, or until cooked through and bubbly. Makes 4 servings.

HEARTY MEAT LASAGNA STACKS

8 ounces	**mild Italian sausage**
1 cup	**marinara sauce**
1 can (6 ounces)	**tomato paste**
1 teaspoon	**garlic powder**
15 ounces	**ricotta cheese**
1	**large egg**
3 cups	**grated mozzarella cheese**
3/4 cup	**grated Parmesan cheese**
36	**refrigerated wonton wrapper squares**

Turn toaster oven to convection bake at 350 degrees (or bake at 375 degrees).

In a large frying pan, saute sausage over medium-high heat until cooked through and lightly browned, about 5 minutes, breaking into small bits as it cooks. Turn off heat and stir in marinara sauce, tomato paste, and garlic powder.

In a small bowl, mix together the ricotta cheese and egg.

Assemble 6 stacks on a baking sheet in layers in the following order: 1 tablespoon sauce in a 3-inch circle; 2 wonton squares (stacked together); about 2 tablespoons ricotta cheese mixture; a generous tablespoon of sauce; a little mozzarella and Parmesan cheese. Repeat for 3 layers in each stack. Bake 25–30 minutes, or until cooked through and bubbly. Serve immediately. Makes 6 servings.

HONEY MUSTARD NUT-CRUSTED SALMON

2 tablespoons	**butter or margarine,** melted
3 tablespoons	**Dijon mustard**
2 tablespoons	**honey**
1/4 cup	**ground or very finely minced pecans**
1/4 cup	**toasted breadcrumbs**
1/4 cup	**finely grated Parmesan cheese**
1 tablespoon	**dried parsley flakes**
4 fillets (4 ounces each)	**salmon**

Turn toaster oven to convection bake at 425 degrees (or bake at 450 degrees).

Mix together butter, mustard, and honey; set aside.

On a salad plate, mix together the nuts, breadcrumbs, cheese, and parsley. Brush tops of salmon fillets with mustard mixture, and then coat tops with crumb mixture; place coated sides up in a shallow baking dish or broiling pan. Bake for 15 minutes on a rack near the top of the oven. Turn toaster oven to broil and then broil for 3–5 minutes, or until browned, watching closely so as not to burn. Makes 4 servings.

TURKEY AND STUFFING ROLLS

1 box (6 ounces)	**stuffing mix**
1 rib	**celery,** leaves included, diced
2 tablespoons	**minced flat-leaf parsley**
2	**cremini mushrooms,** diced
6 (1/4-inch-thick) slices	**deli turkey (about 1/2 pound)**
6 tablespoons	**cranberry sauce**

Turn toaster oven to bake at 375 degrees.

Cook the stuffing mix according to package directions and let cool to warm. Stir in celery, parsley, and mushrooms.

Lay turkey slices on a flat surface and spread 1 tablespoon cranberry sauce on each slice.

Spread some stuffing mixture on each slice of turkey and roll up. Place on an 8 x 11-inch baking sheet prepared with nonstick cooking spray and bake for 30 minutes. Serve immediately. Makes 6 servings.

PARCHMENT PACKET FISH DINNERS

1 tablespoon	**lemon zest**
2 teaspoons	**salt,** divided
1/2 teaspoon	**pepper,** divided
4 fillets (4 ounces each)	**tilapia or other white fish**
4	**baby red or new potatoes,** cut into 1/4-inch-thick slices
1 tablespoon	**butter or margarine**
2 cups	**fresh or frozen pea pods**
1 tablespoon	**minced fresh ginger**
3 cloves	**garlic,** minced
1 cup	**coconut milk**

Turn toaster oven to convection bake at 400 degrees (or bake at 425 degrees).

Stir together the lemon zest, 1 teaspoon salt, and 1/4 teaspoon pepper. Marinate fish with the lemon zest mixture in a ziplock bag at room temperature for about 10 minutes.

Meanwhile, saute the potato slices in butter in a frying pan over medium heat for 3 minutes. Add pea pods, ginger, and garlic and saute 2 minutes more.

Cut some parchment paper into four 6-inch squares. Remove fish from marinade and place a fillet in the center of each parchment square. Spread vegetable mixture evenly over fillets. Ladle a few tablespoons coconut milk over top. Sprinkle with remaining salt and pepper. Fold edges of parchment up over fish and crimp edges to secure. Place packets on an 8 x 11-inch baking sheet. Bake for 30 minutes. Serve immediately, allowing each person to tear open the bag just before eating. Makes 4 servings.

PARMESAN-CRUSTED SALMON CAKES

1 ½ pounds	**salmon fillets**
2 tablespoons	**lemon juice**
2 tablespoons	**mayonnaise**
1 tablespoon	**Dijon mustard**
2	**large eggs**
1 cup	**panko or breadcrumbs**
½	**medium onion,** peeled
2 tablespoons	**minced parsley**
¾ cup	**finely grated Parmesan cheese,** divided

Dice salmon and mix all remaining ingredients except ½ cup Parmesan cheese. Shape mixture into 4-inch circles that are about 1 inch thick. Sprinkle each cake with a little of the remaining Parmesan cheese and press into cakes with fingers. Place on a plate and refrigerate for at least 30 minutes.

Turn toaster oven to convection bake at 425 degrees (or bake at 450 degrees).

Place cakes on an 8 x 11-inch baking sheet prepared with nonstick cooking spray and bake for 20 minutes. Turn cakes over and bake 15–20 minutes more, or until lightly browned. Serve immediately. Makes 6 cakes.

SAUCY CHICKEN THIGHS

1/4 cup	**apricot or peach jam**
1/4 cup	**Dijon mustard**
2 tablespoons	**honey**
1/2 tablespoon	**paprika**
1/2 tablespoon	**curry powder**
1/2 tablespoon	**Worcestershire sauce**
6 to 8	**boneless, skinless chicken thighs**

Turn toaster oven to convection bake at 350 degrees (or bake at 375 degrees).

Mix together all ingredients except chicken. Spread half the sauce in the bottom of a 9-inch square baking pan. Place chicken on top of sauce. Spread remaining sauce over top and then bake, uncovered, for 1 hour. Makes 4–6 servings.

FLANK STEAK PINWHEELS

1 (1 1/2- to 2-pound)	**flank steak**
	salt and pepper
8 ounces	**Provolone cheese slices** (about 10 slices)
1 box (10 ounces)	**frozen spinach,** thawed
1/4 teaspoon	**nutmeg**
2 tablespoons	**cream cheese,** softened
3	**green onions,** very thinly sliced, tops included
	spray canola oil

Place steak on a cutting board, grain running vertical. With a large sturdy knife parallel to the cutting surface, slice flank steak almost in half and open flat, butterfly style. Generously sprinkle with salt and pepper. Lay cheese slices on top of steak, covering entire surface. Squeeze spinach completely dry and then mix with nutmeg and cream cheese. Spread spinach mixture over cheese and then sprinkle green onions over top.

Roll up flank steak away from you, jellyroll style. Cut across grain into 6 (1 1/2-inch-thick) slices. Secure with bamboo skewers. Place slices spiral side up on an 8 x 11-inch baking pan prepared with nonstick cooking spray. Spray tops of slices with oil.

Turn toaster oven to broil at 450 degrees.

Broil 10 minutes, then turn over and broil 8–10 minutes more, or until cooked through. Makes 6 servings.

CHICKEN CONFETTI RICE BAKE

1 tablespoon	**butter or margarine**
4	**skinless chicken thighs**
1/2	**green bell pepper,** diced
1	**medium yellow onion,** diced
3 cloves	**garlic,** minced
1 box (6 ounces)	**long grain and wild rice mix**
1 can (14 ounces)	**chicken broth**
1 can (15 ounces)	**diced tomatoes with liquid**
1 cup	**frozen corn,** thawed

Turn toaster oven to bake at 375 degrees.

In a large frying pan over medium-high heat, melt the butter. Cook chicken thighs, covered, about 5 minutes on each side until well browned. Remove thighs from pan and set aside.

Add bell pepper, onion, garlic, and rice to frying pan and stir and cook 1 minute. Add seasoning packet from box of rice mix. (If there is no seasoning packet, add two teaspoons of seasoned salt.) Add remaining ingredients to pan and bring to a simmer. Pour rice mixture into a 2 1/2-quart baking dish prepared with nonstick cooking spray. Place chicken thighs on top, almost submerging them. Bake 45–50 minutes, or until lightly browned and bubbly around the edges. Makes 4 servings.

QUICK CHICKEN POT PIES

2	**boneless, skinless chicken breasts**
4 tablespoons	**unsalted butter or margarine,** divided
1	**medium russet potato,** peeled and diced
1 bag (12 ounces)	**frozen diced onion, carrot, and celery mix**
1 cup	**frozen peas**
1/4 cup	**flour**
1 cup	**2 percent or whole milk**
	salt and pepper
2 (9-inch)	**refrigerated piecrusts**
1	**large egg,** mixed with 1 tablespoon water

Turn toaster oven to bake at 375 degrees.

Dice chicken breasts into small cubes and then saute chicken in 1 tablespoon butter over medium-high heat until cooked through and lightly browned. Add potato cubes and cook about 3 minutes, stirring. Add frozen vegetables and saute about 1 minute. Add remaining butter. Stir in flour and cook until flour is absorbed. Add milk and cook a few minutes, stirring until thickened. Remove from heat and season with salt and pepper to taste.

Fill 6 (8- to 10-ounce) ramekins, with mixture almost to top. Cut piecrusts to fit tops and place on top of each ramekin. Make a few slits with a knife in top of each crust. Brush with egg wash. Bake for 25–30 minutes, or until bubbly and browned. Makes 6 servings.

CAESAR CHICKEN FILLETS

4	**boneless, skinless chicken breasts**
1/4 cup	**Caesar salad dressing**
1 cup	**Caesar-style croutons**
1/4 cup	**grated Parmesan cheese**
1 tablespoon	**canola oil,** divided

Turn toaster oven to convection bake at 375 degrees (or bake at 400 degrees).

Cut each chicken breast into two large planks lengthwise and then brush with a thin coating of salad dressing.

Crush croutons to fine crumbs and then mix with the cheese. Press chicken planks into crouton mixture on all sides. Pour 1/2 tablespoon oil into an 8 x 11-inch baking pan. Place 4 of the chicken planks in the pan and bake 20 minutes. Turn chicken over and bake 15–20 minutes more, or until crust is lightly browned and crispy. Repeat with remaining chicken planks. Serve immediately. Makes 4–6 servings.

HAM AND POTATO GRATIN

3	**medium russet potatoes,** peeled
1 (4-ounce) slice	**ham,** diced
2 cups	**grated Gruyère, Fontina, or cheddar cheese**
1 jar (15 ounces)	**alfredo sauce**
3 tablespoons	**minced parsley**
1/2	**medium onion,** peeled and minced

Turn toaster oven to bake at 375 degrees.

Slice potatoes into 1/8-inch-thick slices, place on a plate, and cover with plastic wrap. Microwave on high for 5 minutes.

In a 2 1/2-quart pan, layer as you would a lasagna using one-third of the following: potato slices, ham, cheese, Alfredo sauce, parsley, and onion. Repeat to make two more layers. Bake for 45–50 minutes, or until golden brown and bubbly. Let stand 5 minutes before serving. Makes 4–6 servings.

BAKED CHICKEN CURRY

2 pounds	**boneless, skinless chicken breasts**
1/4 cup	**unsalted butter or margarine**
1	**medium carrot,** peeled and diced
1	**medium russet potato,** peeled and diced
2 tablespoons	**flour**
1 tablespoon	**curry powder**
2 tablespoons	**creamy peanut butter**
1 tablespoon	**rice vinegar**
2 cups	**half-and-half**
	Tabasco sauce, to taste
4 cups	**cooked rice**

Turn toaster oven to bake at 350 degrees.

Cut chicken into 1/2-inch cubes and saute in a large frying pan with butter over medium-high heat until cooked through and slightly browned on outside edges. Add carrot and potato and saute until vegetables are fork tender. Stir in flour until absorbed.

In a bowl, mix together the curry powder, peanut butter, vinegar, half-and-half, and Tabasco sauce. Stir into pan and remove from heat. Spread rice in a 2 1/2-quart baking dish and spread chicken mixture on top. Bake for 15–20 minutes, or until lightly browned and bubbly. Serve immediately. Makes 4–6 servings.

CHICKEN NACHOS CASSEROLE

2 cups	**broken corn tortilla chips,** divided
1 jar (16 ounces)	**salsa**
1 cup	**frozen corn**
1 can (15 ounces)	**black beans,** drained
1/2 cup	**light sour cream**
1	**jalapeño,** minced
2 tablespoons	**flour**
1 cup	**grated Monterey Jack cheese**
2 1/2 cups	**cooked and cubed chicken**
1 cup	**grated cheddar cheese**

Turn toaster oven to bake at 400 degrees.

Place half of the chips in the bottom of a 9-inch square baking pan.

Stir together the salsa, corn, beans, sour cream, jalapeño, flour, and Monterey Jack cheese. Spoon mixture over chips. Bake for 25 minutes. Remove from oven and sprinkle with remaining tortilla chips and cheddar cheese. Return to toaster oven and bake 10 minutes more, watching closely so as not to burn, until cheese melts. Serve immediately, garnished with additional jalapeño and sour cream, if desired. Makes 4–6 servings.

CRUSTY FISH FILLETS

1/2 cup	**sour cream**
1 tablespoon	**Dijon mustard**
1 cup	**panko or breadcrumbs**
1/2 cup	**finely grated Parmesan cheese**
2 tablespoons	**minced flat-leaf parsley**
4 fillets (1 inch thick each)	**cod or other sturdy white fish**

Turn toaster oven to convection bake at 400 degrees (or bake at 425 degrees).

Mix sour cream and mustard together. Mix together the panko or breadcrumbs, Parmesan, and parsley, and then spread on a small plate. Coat fish in sour cream mixture and then press both sides of coated fish into crumb mixture. Place a wire rack on an 8 x 11-inch baking sheet and spray with nonstick cooking spray. Place fish on wire rack. Bake 20–22 minutes, or until cooked through and lightly browned. Makes 4 servings.

GARLIC HERB PORK CHOPS

3 cloves	**garlic**
1/2 teaspoon	**salt**
1 tablespoon	**minced rosemary**
1 tablespoon	**minced flat-leaf parsley**
1/2 tablespoon	**minced thyme leaves**
2 tablespoons	**olive oil**
4 (1-inch-thick)	**pork chops**

Turn toaster oven to broil at 450 degrees.

Mince and then mash the garlic and salt with the widest part of the blade of a large knife. Stir in the herbs and oil. Rub this mixture over all the pork chops.

Broil chops on an 8 x 11-inch baking sheet prepared with nonstick cooking spray in the middle of the oven for 8–10 minutes, watching closely so as not to burn. Turn over and broil 5 minutes more, or until browned. Let stand 5 minutes before serving. Makes 4 servings.

VEGGIE MAIN DISHES

SHORTCUT TAMALE PIE

2 cans (15 ounces each)	**chili with beans**
1/4 cup	**tomato paste**
1 can (4 ounces)	**sliced black olives,** drained
1 cup	**frozen corn**
3	**green onions,** thinly sliced
2 cups	**grated sharp cheddar cheese,** divided
2 cups	**water**
1 teaspoon	**salt**
3/4 cup	**cornmeal**

Turn toaster oven to bake at 375 degrees.

Stir together chili, tomato paste, olives, corn, onions, and all but 1/2 cup cheese. Spread mixture in a 2 1/2-quart baking pan sprayed with nonstick cooking spray. Sprinkle remaining cheese on top.

In a medium saucepan, bring water and salt to a boil. Slowly add cornmeal while whisking continuously to prevent lumps. Cook 2–3 minutes, or until thickened. Spread cornmeal mixture over chili mixture. Bake for 35–40 minutes, or until cornmeal topping is set and chili mixture is bubbling. Serve immediately. Makes 4–6 servings.

SUBLIME SPINACH LASAGNA STACKS

1 jar (16 ounces)	**Alfredo sauce**
1/4 cup	**flour**
1 teaspoon	**garlic powder**
15 ounces	**ricotta cheese**
1	**large egg**
48	**refrigerated wonton wrapper squares**
1 box (10 ounces)	**frozen chopped spinach,** thawed and drained
3 cups	**grated mozzarella cheese**
3/4 cup	**grated Parmesan cheese**

Turn toaster oven to convection bake at 350 degrees (or bake at 375 degrees).

Stir together Alfredo sauce, flour, and garlic powder. In a small bowl, mix together the ricotta cheese and egg.

Assemble 6 stacks on a baking sheet in layers in the following order: 1 tablespoon sauce in a 3-inch circle; 2 wonton squares (stacked together); about 2 tablespoons ricotta cheese mixture; a generous tablespoon sauce; some spinach; and some mozzarella and Parmesan cheese. Repeat for 4 layers in each stack. Bake 45–50 minutes, or until cooked through and bubbly. Serve immediately. Makes 6 servings.

MEDITERRANEAN STUFFED PEPPERS

1 box (4 ounces)	**long grain and wild rice mix**
3	**bell peppers,** any color
1	**medium yellow onion,** diced
1 tablespoon	**canola oil**
1 cup	**diced cremini mushrooms**
1/2 cup	**crumbled feta cheese**
1/2 cup	**diced Italian flat-leaf parsley**
1/2 cup	**Italian-style tomato paste**
1/2 cup	**water**
2 tablespoons	**extra virgin olive oil**

Cook the rice mix according to package directions, including seasoning packet; set aside to cool. (If there is no seasoning packet, add seasoned salt to taste.)

Cut bell peppers in half lengthwise and remove seeds. Blanch in boiling water for 3 minutes and then remove from water and set cut side up on an 8 x 11-inch baking sheet.

Turn toaster oven to convection bake at 350 degrees (or bake at 375 degrees).

Saute the onion in canola oil in a large skillet over medium-high heat until cooked through. Add the mushrooms and cook until softened, about 2 minutes. Remove from heat and stir in cooked rice, cheese, and parsley. Spoon mixture into pepper halves.

In a bowl, stir together the tomato paste, water, and oil. Drizzle over stuffed peppers. Bake for 35–40 minutes, or until cooked through and bubbly. Makes 4–6 servings.

HARVEST STUFFED ZUCCHINI

4	**medium zucchinis,** cut in half lengthwise with ends trimmed
1 tablespoon	**unsalted butter or margarine**
1	**medium yellow onion,** diced
2 cloves	**garlic,** minced
1 box (10 ounces)	**frozen chopped spinach,** thawed and drained
1/2 teaspoon	**poultry seasoning**
	salt and pepper
2 slices	**whole-grain or multigrain bread**
1	**large egg**
2 tablespoons	**sour cream**
1/2 cup	**grated Parmesan cheese,** divided

Turn toaster oven to bake at 350 degrees.

With a spoon, scoop out the middle seedy part of each zucchini.

Heat a frying pan to medium-high heat. Melt the butter and then saute the onion and garlic for 1–2 minutes, or until onion is translucent. Add spinach, and seasonings. Remove from heat.

Pulse bread in a food processor until large crumbs. Stir crumbs into vegetable mixture. Stir in egg, sour cream, and half the Parmesan cheese. Spoon this mixture into hollowed out zucchini pieces and press down to secure. Place on an 8 x 11-inch pan and cover with aluminum foil; bake for 12–15 minutes. Remove foil, sprinkle with remaining cheese and cook 5–8 minutes more, or until cheese is melted. Makes 4–6 servings.

DOUBLE-SAUCED BAKED PASTA

1 cup	**grape tomatoes**
1 tablespoon	**extra virgin olive oil**
2 teaspoons	**garlic powder**
1 bag (8 ounces)	**ziti or penne pasta,** cooked al dente and rinsed
4 ounces	**mild Italian sausage,** cooked and crumbled
1/2 cup	**diced flat-leaf parsley,** divided
2 cups	**marinara sauce**
3/4 cup	**Gorgonzola cheese,** crumbled
3/4 cup	**grated Parmesan cheese**
1 cup	**sour cream**

Turn toaster oven to broil.

Toss the tomatoes in oil and spread on an edged 8 x 11-inch baking sheet. Sprinkle with garlic powder and broil on middle oven rack for 3–5 minutes, or until tomatoes split and are lightly browned, watching closely so as not to burn.

In a large bowl, toss the pasta, sausage, most of the parsley, tomato mixture, and marinara sauce. Spread in a 2 1/2-quart baking dish that has been generously sprayed with nonstick cooking spray. Sprinkle remaining parsley over top.

Turn toaster oven to bake at 350 degrees.

Stir cheeses into sour cream and spread over pasta mixture, covering entire surface. Bake for 25–30 minutes, or until heated through and bubbly. Serve immediately. Makes 4–6 servings.

BLACK BEAN EMPANADAS

1/2	**red bell pepper,** diced
3	**green onions,** thinly sliced
1 tablespoon	**butter or margarine**
2 cans (15 ounces each)	**black beans,** drained
1 teaspoon	**cumin**
1 teaspoon	**chili powder**
1/2 teaspoon	**salt**
1/2 cup	**grated cheddar cheese**
2 cloves	**garlic,** diced
1/4 cup	**diced cilantro**
2 (9-inch)	**refrigerated piecrusts**
1	**large egg,** mixed with 1 tablespoon water

Turn toaster oven to bake at 375 degrees.

Saute bell pepper and onions in butter for 1–2 minutes, or until softened. Turn off heat and stir in black beans, spices, salt, cheese, garlic, and cilantro.

Cut each piecrust in half. Evenly divide bean mixture and place a portion on one side of each piecrust half. Brush a little egg wash around edges of piecrusts. Fold uncovered crust over top and crimp edges together with a fork. Brush tops of empanadas with egg wash. Place empanadas in a single layer on an 8 x 11-inch baking sheet prepared with nonstick cooking spray and bake for 15–18 minutes, or until golden brown. Bake remaining empanadas in same way. Makes 4 servings.

CHILE CHEESE CASSEROLE

1 tablespoon	**canola oil**
1 can (26 ounces)	**roasted peeled green chiles,** drained
3 cups	**grated Monterey Jack cheese**
4 to 6	**green onions,** thinly sliced, tops included
6	**large eggs**
1 cup	**milk**
1 teaspoon	**chile powder**
1 teaspoon	**cumin**
1 teaspoon	**salt**

Turn toaster oven to bake at 350 degrees.

Pour oil in the bottom of a 9-inch square baking pan. Make a layer using one-third of the chiles to completely cover the bottom of pan. Sprinkle half the cheese and half the onions over chiles. Lay another third of the chiles on top. Sprinkle remaining cheese and onions on top. Finish with remaining chiles.

Beat eggs with milk, spices, and salt. Pour egg mixture over top. Bake 35–40 minutes, or until lightly browned and bubbly. Let stand for 5 minutes before serving. Makes 4–6 servings.

TOASTER OVEN CHIMICHANGAS

3	**green onions,** thinly sliced, tops included
1	**Anaheim chile,** seeds and pulp removed, diced
1 tablespoon	**unsalted butter or margarine**
1 can (14 ounces)	**black beans,** drained
1/2 cup	**fresh or frozen corn**
2 cups	**grated cheddar or Monterey Jack cheese**
1/2 tablespoon	**cumin**
1/2 tablespoon	**chile powder**
6 small (6- to 7-inch)	**flour tortillas**
	canola oil spray

Turn toaster oven to convection bake at 375 degrees (or bake at 400 degrees).

Saute the onions and chile in butter over medium-high heat for 3–5 minutes until softened. Stir in beans and corn and then remove from heat. Stir in cheese and spices.

Spoon 1/2 cup of the mixture onto each tortilla and then roll up, burrito style. Place in a single layer on an 8 x 11-inch baking sheet prepared with nonstick cooking spray. Generously spray each tortilla bundle with oil. Bake for 20–25 minutes, or until golden brown. Makes 6 servings.

SHORTCUT DINNER FRITTATA

2 tablespoons	**olive oil**
$\frac{1}{2}$	**yellow onion,** diced
3 cloves	**garlic,** minced
$\frac{1}{2}$	**red bell pepper,** diced
1 box (10 ounces)	**frozen chopped spinach,** thawed and squeezed dry
	salt and pepper
$\frac{1}{4}$ teaspoon	**nutmeg**
8	**large eggs**
$\frac{1}{2}$ cup	**cream**
$\frac{3}{4}$ cup	**grated Parmesan cheese**
$\frac{1}{2}$ cup	**crumbled feta cheese**

Turn toaster oven to bake at 375 degrees.

Preheat a 9-inch square baking pan for 20 minutes. Pour oil in pan. Scatter onion, garlic, and bell pepper on top. Toss spinach with a little salt, pepper, and nutmeg. Sprinkle spinach mixture on top.

In a bowl, whisk together eggs, cream, and Parmesan cheese. Pour egg mixture over spinach mixture. Sprinkle feta cheese on top, pressing into egg mixture. Bake 35–40 minutes, or until lightly browned on top. Makes 4–6 servings.

SAVORY ITALIAN BREAD PUDDING

1 jar (6 ounces)	**sun-dried tomatoes in oil**
1 cup	**diced yellow onion**
1 cup	**diced zucchini**
1	**small loaf day-old French bread,** cut into 1-inch cubes (about 6 cups)
1 1/2 cups	**grated mozzarella cheese**
3/4 cup	**grated Parmesan cheese**
1/3 cup	**chopped basil or flat-leaf parsley**
1 tablespoon	**extra virgin olive oil**
6	**large eggs**
2 cups	**whole milk**
1 teaspoon	**salt**
1 teaspoon	**white pepper**
1/4 teaspoon	**nutmeg**

Turn toaster oven to bake at 375 degrees.

Drain oil from jar of tomatoes and reserve 2 tablespoons. Pour 1 tablespoon oil into a medium frying pan. Saute onion over medium-high heat until lightly browned, but not soft, about 3 minutes. Add zucchini and saute 2 minutes more. Dice the tomatoes and stir into pan. Pour remaining oil into a 2 1/2-quart casserole dish. Toss together the bread cubes, sauteed vegetables, most of the cheese, and parsley. Place in casserole and sprinkle remaining cheese over top.

In a bowl, stir together the eggs, milk, and spices and pour over bread mixture, pressing down to make sure all bread cubes are soaked. Bake for 45–50 minutes, or until almost firm in center and browned on top. Let stand 10 minutes before serving. Makes 4–6 servings.

WEEKNIGHT RATATOUILLE

2	**red bell peppers,** cut into 1-inch strips
1 tablespoon	**olive oil**
1 can (6 ounces)	**tomato paste**
1 cup	**heavy cream**
1 teaspoon	**salt**
2 cups	**thinly sliced zucchini**
2 cups	**thinly sliced yellow squash**
1 cup	**thinly sliced eggplant**
1	**small yellow onion,** thinly sliced
1 cup	**grated Gruyère or Parmesan cheese**

Turn toaster oven to broil at 450 degrees.

Brush skin side of pepper strips with oil and then broil skin side up for 3–5 minutes, watching closely so as not to burn; remove and set aside. Turn oven down to bake at 375 degrees.

In a blender, blend the roasted pepper strips, tomato paste, cream, and salt until smooth.

Layer in a 2 1/2-quart baking pan prepared with nonstick cooking spray in the following order: one-third of the vegetables, half the sauce, another third of the vegetables, remaining sauce, and remaining vegetables.

Bake, uncovered, for about 1 hour, or until bubbly around the edges. Remove from oven, sprinkle cheese on top, turn toaster oven back to broil and broil 3–5 minutes, or until cheese is browned and bubbly. Serve immediately. Makes 4–6 servings.

CHEESY MUSHROOM CANNELLONI

1	**medium onion,** diced
1 tablespoon	**unsalted butter or margarine**
2 cups	**chopped cremini mushrooms**
2 cups	**marinara sauce,** divided
1 1/2 cups	**grated mozzarella cheese**
1/2 cup	**ricotta cheese**
16	**refrigerated egg roll wrappers**
1 cup	**Alfredo sauce**
1/4 cup	**finely grated Parmesan cheese**

Turn toaster oven to bake at 350 degrees.

Saute onion in a frying pan with butter over medium-high heat for about 2 minutes. Add mushrooms and cook 2–3 minutes, or until most of the liquid has evaporated. Turn off heat and stir in 1 cup marinara sauce, mozzarella, and ricotta.

Lay two egg roll wrappers stacked together on a flat surface. Spoon 1/4 cup mushroom mixture on top about 1 inch from one edge. Roll up, enchilada style. Repeat with remaining egg roll wrappers until you have 8 total rolls. Spread remaining marinara sauce in a 9-inch square baking pan. Place the cannelloni rolls on top of the marinara sauce as necessary to make a single layer in the pan. Spread Alfredo sauce evenly over top. Sprinkle Parmesan cheese on top. Bake for 30–35 minutes, or until lightly browned and bubbly. Let stand 5 minutes before serving. Makes 4–6 servings.

PARMESAN POLENTA CAKES

1 tube (32 ounces)	**precooked polenta**
6 tablespoons	**finely grated Parmesan cheese**
1	**medium yellow onion,** diced
1	**medium zucchini,** diced
6 to 8	**cremini mushrooms,** diced
2 tablespoons	**canola oil**
2 cups	**marinara sauce**

Turn toaster oven to broil at 450 degrees.

Cut polenta into 6 (1-inch-thick) slices. Place rounds on an 8 x 11-inch baking sheet prepared with nonstick cooking spray and broil for 5–7 minutes, or until lightly browned on top. Turn rounds over and spread 1 tablespoon Parmesan cheese on top of each. Broil 5–7 minutes more, or until cheese is crusty and lightly browned.

Meanwhile, saute vegetables in oil in a frying pan over medium-high heat until softened. Stir in marinara sauce and heat until bubbly. Serve spooned over the cooked polenta rounds. Makes 4–6 servings.

CHEESY CORN PUDDING

4 ounces	**Monterey Jack cheese**
4 ounces	**cheddar cheese**
3	**large eggs,** beaten
1 cup	**light sour cream**
1/2 cup	**cornmeal**
1/2 cup	**butter or margarine,** melted
1 can (8 ounces)	**cream-style corn**
1 can (7 ounces)	**whole kernel corn,** drained
1/2 teaspoon	**Worcestershire sauce**

Turn toaster oven to bake at 350 degrees.

Cut cheeses into 1/4-inch cubes. Stir all ingredients together. Spread mixture in a 2 1/2-quart baking dish prepared with a generous amount of nonstick cooking spray.

Bake for 45–50 minutes, or until almost set in center and golden brown. Let stand for 5 minutes before serving. Makes 4–6 servings.

DESSERTS

EASY APPLE DUMPLINGS

2	**medium Granny Smith apples,** cored and peeled
2	**medium Golden Delicious apples,** cored and peeled
1 tablespoon	**butter or margarine**
1/2 teaspoon	**cinnamon**
1/4 teaspoon	**nutmeg**
1 jar (12 ounces)	**caramel sauce,** divided
1/3 cup	**diced walnuts or pecans**
1 box (17 ounces)	**frozen puff pastry,** thawed
1	**large egg,** mixed with 1 tablespoon water

Turn toaster oven to convection bake at 350 degrees (or bake at 375 degrees).

Slice apples into 1/4-inch slices and saute in butter in a large frying pan over medium-high heat for about 3 minutes, or until most of liquid has evaporated. Remove from heat and stir in spices, 1/3 cup caramel sauce, and nuts.

Place pastry sheets on a flat surface and cut each sheet into four squares. Divide apple mixture into 8 portions and mound one portion on each square of pastry. Brush egg wash around edges of pastry squares. Bring opposite corners of each square to top over the apple mixture. Twist corners together to seal. Brush each dumpling with egg wash.

Bake for 18–20 minutes, or until golden brown. Heat remaining caramel sauce and drizzle over tops of dumplings. Serve immediately. Makes 8 servings.

QUICK BERRY CAKE

1 cup	**sugar,** divided
1 cup	**flour**
1 teaspoon	**baking powder**
1/2 teaspoon	**salt**
1 cup	**milk**
1/2 cup	**unsalted butter or margarine,** melted
2 cups	**frozen berries**

Turn toaster oven to bake at 350 degrees.

Stir together 3/4 cup sugar, flour, baking powder, salt, and milk. Stir in butter until batter is smooth with only very small lumps remaining. Pour mixture into a 9-inch square baking pan prepared with nonstick cooking spray. Sprinkle frozen berries on top. Sprinkle remaining sugar over berries. Bake for 45–50 minutes, or until golden brown and bubbly. Serve immediately with whipped cream or ice cream, if desired. Makes 4–6 servings.

APRICOT PINEAPPLE PASTRIES

1 box (17 ounces)	**frozen puff pastry,** thawed
1 jar (8 ounces)	**apricot-pineapple jam**
1 package (8 ounces)	**light cream cheese,** softened
1/3 cup	**sugar**
1/2 teaspoon	**cinnamon**
1/4 teaspoon	**nutmeg**

Turn toaster oven to convection bake at 350 degrees (or bake at 375 degrees).

Cut each pastry sheet into 4 squares. Spread 1 tablespoon jam in center of each square, leaving 2 inches around edges of pastry. Spoon 1 tablespoon cream cheese on top of jam. Make a cut from the corners of each square to the jam. Fold corners over jam mixture, pinching at the center. Mix together sugar, cinnamon, and nutmeg. Brush each pastry with a little water and then sprinkle generously with sugar mixture. Bake for 15–18 minutes, or until golden brown. Serve immediately. Makes 8 pastries.

GINGERSNAP APPLE CRISP

1 cup	**flour**
1 cup	**sugar,** divided
4 tablespoons	**chilled unsalted butter or margarine**
1 1/2 cups	**diced walnuts or pecans**
1 1/2 cups	**finely crumbled gingersnap cookies**
2 cups	**peeled and sliced Granny Smith apples** (1/4 inch slices)
1 tablespoon	**cornstarch**

Turn toaster oven to bake at 350 degrees.

Place flour and 2/3 cup sugar in a bowl and cut in butter with a pastry blender or fork until small crumbs. Stir in nuts and gingersnap crumbles.

Toss apples with remaining sugar and cornstarch. Stir in 1/2 cup gingersnap mixture.

Spoon apple mixture into a 2 1/2-quart baking dish prepared with nonstick cooking spray. Spread remaining gingersnap mixture on top. Bake for 30–35 minutes, or until bubbly. Let cool 15 minutes before serving. Makes 4–6 servings.

CHOCOLATE BREAD PUDDING CUPS

1 cup	**whole milk**
2 tablespoons	**sugar**
1 tablespoon	**unsweetened cocoa powder**
1 teaspoon	**vanilla**
2	**large eggs**
2 cups	**cubed (1/2-inch) day-old Challah bread**
4 ounces	**semisweet chocolate,** coarsely chopped, divided
2 tablespoons	**unsalted butter or margarine**

Combine milk, sugar, cocoa powder, vanilla, and eggs. Add bread cubes and toss gently. Cover and chill up to 4 hours.

Turn toaster oven to bake at 350 degrees.

Toss bread mixture with half of the chocolate. Generously butter 4 (8- to 10-ounce) ramekins. Place a generous 1/2 cup of bread mixture into each ramekin. Sprinkle remaining chocolate on top. Bake for 30–35 minutes, or until puffed and firm in centers. Makes 4 servings.

SHORTCUT APPLE STRUDEL

5 sheets	**frozen phyllo dough,** thawed
6 tablespoons	**unsalted butter or margarine,** melted, divided
1/4 cup	**sugar,** divided
1/2 cup	**raisins,** diced
1/3 cup	**toasted breadcrumbs**
1	**Granny Smith apple,** peeled and cored
1	**Golden Delicious apple,** peeled and cored
1/2 tablespoon	**lemon juice**
1/2 teaspoon	**cinnamon**
1/4 teaspoon	**salt**
1/4 teaspoon	**nutmeg**
1/4 cup	**finely chopped walnuts**

Turn toaster oven to convection bake at 425 degrees (or bake at 450 degrees).

Lay 1 layer of phyllo on a flat surface. Brush with 1 tablespoon butter and then sprinkle with 1 teaspoon sugar. Repeat for a total of 5 sheets and then stack together. Mix together remaining sugar and all remaining ingredients except butter.

Spread half the apple mixture along the long edge of the stacked phyllo. Roll jellyroll style from long edge. Slice into 2-inch slices and place in a single layer on an 8 x 11-inch baking sheet prepared with nonstick cooking spray, spiral side up. Brush with remaining butter. Bake 12–15 minutes, or until browned. Let stand 30 minutes before serving. Makes 6–8 servings.

PEAR ALMOND RUSTIC TARTS

1 box (17 ounces)	**frozen puff pastry,** thawed
1/2 cup	**almond paste**
1/4 cup	**sour cream**
2	**ripe Bartlett pears,** peeled
1/2 cup	**apple jelly,** melted
1/3 cup	**sugar**
1/2 teaspoon	**cinnamon**
1/4 teaspoon	**nutmeg**
1/4 teaspoon	**salt**

Turn toaster oven to convection bake at 400 degrees (or bake at 425 degrees).

Spread the pastry sheets on a flat surface and cut each sheet into 2 rectangles width wise. Mix together the almond paste and sour cream and spread some of the mixture in the center of each rectangle, leaving 2 inches around the edges.

Slice pears into 1/4-inch slices and spread on top of almond mixture. Brush tops of pear slices with jelly. Mix together remaining ingredients and sprinkle on top of pears. Fold bare edges over pear mixture, forming a crust around edges. Bake in two batches on an 8 x 11-inch baking sheet for 22–25 minutes, or until golden brown. Serve immediately. Makes 4 servings.

QUICK CHOCOLATE SOUFFLÉS

1/2 cup	**sugar,** divided
1/4 cup	**flour**
1/4 cup	**dark cocoa powder**
1/4 teaspoon	**salt**
2 tablespoons	**unsalted butter or margarine**
1 cup	**whole milk**
1/2 cup	**semisweet chocolate chips**
4	**large eggs,** separated
1/2 teaspoon	**cream of tartar**

Turn toaster oven to bake at 400 degrees.

Stir together 1/4 cup sugar, flour, cocoa powder, and salt. Cut in butter with a fork or pastry blender until fine crumbs.

Bring milk to a simmer in a small saucepan. Gradually whisk in cocoa powder mixture and chocolate chips, cooking about 1 minute, or until butter is melted and mixture is thickened slightly. Remove from heat. Whisk 3 tablespoons cocoa mixture, one at a time, into the egg yolks. Then whisk entire egg yolk mixture into the cocoa mixture.

Beat egg whites in a mixer with cream of tartar until soft peaks form. Slowly add remaining sugar, beating until stiff peaks. Fold egg whites into cocoa mixture. Spray 4 (1-cup) ramekins with nonstick cooking spray. Add 3/4 cup batter to each ramekin. Bake for 15–18 minutes, or until set. Serve immediately, dusted with powdered sugar if desired. Makes 4 servings.

MINI PUMPKIN CHEESECAKES

1 cup	**graham cracker crumbs**
1/2 cup	**sugar,** divided
2 tablespoons	**butter or margarine,** melted
2 packages (8 ounces each)	**light cream cheese,** softened
1/2 cup	**canned pumpkin**
1 teaspoon	**vanilla**
1/2 teaspoon	**cinnamon**
1/4 teaspoon	**nutmeg**
2	**large eggs**

Turn toaster oven to bake at 350 degrees.

Mix together the graham cracker crumbs, 1 tablespoon sugar, and butter. Press 3 tablespoons of mixture into the bottoms of 6 (8- to 10-ounce) ramekins. Bake for 10 minutes and remove and let cool.

Meanwhile, beat together the remaining sugar and all other ingredients until smooth.

Pour on top of graham cracker crusts in ramekins. Bake for 15–18 minutes, or until almost set in center. Let cool and then refrigerate for at least 2 hours before serving. Makes 6 servings.

RUSTIC APPLE PIE

1	**medium Granny Smith apple,** peeled and cored
1	**medium Golden Delicious apple,** peeled and cored
1 tablespoon	**lemon juice**
2 tablespoons	**cornstarch**
1/2 cup	**sugar**
1/2 teaspoon	**cinnamon**
1/4 teaspoon	**nutmeg**
1/4 teaspoon	**salt**
1 (9-inch)	**refrigerated piecrust**
1	**large egg,** mixed with 1 tablespoon water

Turn toaster oven to bake at 350 degrees.

Slice apples into 1/4-inch slices and toss with lemon juice. Mix together cornstarch, sugar, spices, and salt and stir into apple slices. Place piecrust on an 8 x 11-inch baking sheet prepared with nonstick cooking spray. Mound apple mixture in center on piecrust, leaving about 3 inches around the edge. Fold up edges toward center over apple mixture, crimping together as you go. Brush piecrust edge with egg wash. Bake for 30–35 minutes, or until bubbly and golden brown. Makes 4–6 servings.

ULTIMATE CRUMB CAKE

2 cups	**flour**
1 teaspoon	**baking soda**
1 teaspoon	**baking powder**
1/4 teaspoon	**salt**
1/2 cup	**unsalted butter or margarine**
1 cup	**sugar**
3	**large eggs**
1 teaspoon	**vanilla**
1 cup	**sour cream**

Streusel topping:

1/2 cup	**light brown sugar**
1/4 cup	**unsalted butter or margarine**
1/4 cup	**flour**
1/2 teaspoon	**cinnamon**
1/2 cup	**diced walnuts**

Turn toaster oven to bake at 350 degrees.

Stir together flour, baking soda, baking powder, and salt. Mix together the sugar, eggs, vanilla, and sour cream and then fold into dry ingredients. Pour into a 9-inch square baking pan prepared with nonstick cooking spray.

To make the streusel, mix together to large crumb stage the brown sugar, butter, flour, cinnamon, and walnuts. Top batter with streusel topping, pressing into batter randomly with fingertips. Bake 35–40 minutes, or until set in the center. Makes 4–6 servings.

CARROT MINI CAKES

4	**large carrots,** peeled
1 1/2 cups	**flour**
2 teaspoons	**baking powder**
1/2 teaspoon	**baking soda**
1/2 teaspoon	**salt**
1 teaspoon	**ground cinnamon**
1/2 teaspoon	**allspice**
3/4 cup	**canola oil**
3	**large eggs**
1 cup	**light brown sugar**
1 teaspoon	**vanilla**

Turn toaster oven to bake at 350 degrees.

Grate carrots on small holes on a box grater, enough to make 2 cups. Stir together flour, baking powder, baking soda, salt, and spices. Mix together all remaining ingredients and then stir wet ingredients into dry ingredients. Coat 6 (8- to 10-ounce) ramekins with butter and then a little flour. Pour batter into each ramekin, filling three-fourths full. Bake for 25–30 minutes, or until firm in centers. Cool a few minutes and then carefully invert onto serving plates. Top with cream cheese frosting, whipped cream, or powdered sugar, if desired. Makes 6 servings.

CHOCOLATE SWIRL CHEESECAKE

1 1/2 cups	**chocolate cookie crumbs**
4 tablespoons	**unsalted butter or margarine,** melted
2 packages (8 ounces each)	**cream cheese,** softened
1/2 cup	**sugar**
1 teaspoon	**vanilla**
1/2 cup	**light sour cream**
2	**large eggs**
1 cup	**semisweet chocolate chips,** melted

Turn toaster oven to bake at 325 degrees.

Stir cookie crumbs with butter. Press cookie crumbs into bottom and sides of a 9-inch pie pan.

Beat the cream cheese and sugar with a mixer until well blended. Add vanilla, sour cream, and eggs. Remove 2/3 cup batter and set aside. Stir melted chocolate into remaining batter. Pour chocolate batter into pie pan. Place mounds of reserved white batter into pie pan, and then swirl into the chocolate batter with a knife. Bake 40–45 minutes, or until center is almost set. Turn off oven and let sit in oven until cooled. Refrigerate 2 hours or more, up to overnight. Makes 6–8 servings.

HAZELNUT PEAR POUND CAKE STACKS

1	**small purchased pound cake**
1/2 cup	**diced hazelnuts**
2	**Bartlett or Anjou pears,** peeled and cored
2 tablespoons	**unsalted butter or margarine**
3/4 cup	**Nutella spread**

Turn toaster oven to toast at medium setting.

Slice the cake into 6 (1/2-inch-thick) slices. Place slices directly on a wire rack in the oven and toast for 5–8 minutes, or until crispy and lightly browned. Place hazelnuts on an 8 x 11-inch baking sheet and toast for about 5 minutes, stirring once after 2 minutes.

Slice pears into 1/4-inch-thick slices. Saute in butter over medium-high heat for about 3 minutes, or until cooked through and lightly browned. Place each slice of cake on a serving plate and layer as follows: 2 tablespoons Nutella, some pear slices, and a generous tablespoon of hazelnuts. Serve immediately. Makes 6 servings.

KEY LIME SQUARES

2 cups	**crushed vanilla wafers**
3 tablespoons	**melted butter or margarine**
1 cup	**frozen limeade,** thawed
2 containers (6 ounces each)	**key lime yogurt**
1 small box	**instant vanilla pudding mix**
1 teaspoon	**lime zest**
3 or 4 drops	**green food coloring**
8 ounces	**frozen whipped topping,** thawed

Turn toaster oven to bake at 350 degrees.

Stir together cookie crumbs and butter. Press into the bottom of a 9-inch square baking pan. Bake 10–12 minutes, or until lightly browned.

Mix together the limeade and yogurt. Whisk in pudding mix, lime zest, and food coloring and set aside to thicken for 10 minutes. Gently stir in whipped topping. Spread mixture over crust and refrigerate for 2 hours, or up to overnight. Cut into squares to serve. Makes 6–9 servings.

NOTES

NOTES

NOTES

NOTES

METRIC CONVERSION CHART

Volume Measurements

U.S.	Metric
1 teaspoon	5 ml
1 tablespoon	15 ml
1/4 cup	60 ml
1/3 cup	75 ml
1/2 cup	125 ml
2/3 cup	150 ml
3/4 cup	175 ml
1 cup	250 ml

Weight Measurements

U.S.	Metric
1/2 ounce	15 g
1 ounce	30 g
3 ounces	90 g
4 ounces	115 g
8 ounces	225 g
12 ounces	350 g
1 pound	450 g
2 1/4 pounds	1 kg

Temperature Conversion

Fahrenheit	Celsius
250	120
300	150
325	160
350	180
375	190
400	200
425	220
450	230